अवर फर्स्ट ऐंड फॉरेवर लव

राहुल बी आर

क्रम-सूची

क्रम-सूची

क्रम-सूची

About Words Of Soul Publication

Words of Soul is a writing Community, where we have a group of new budding writers with their talent of framing emotions into words.

Formed by Dr. Nikita Dudagi and Lucky Pandey on May 15th 2021 to encourage and appreciate the enthusiastic writers. Weekly Special events and programs are being conducted to recognise the best Writer of the community. Words of Soul, a Group of Aspiring writers who ink the emotions of their heart to inspire the reader's mind.

Words of Soul Publications is not only a publication, it's a kind of family of writers which includes Co-author, writer, Author, compiler, co- compiler, Graphic Team, Project Heads, CEO, co-founder and Founder. Here Everyone is free to give their ideas and we initiate their actions.

About The Book

The book "OUR FIRST AND FOREVER LOVE" upholds the beauty of our first love towards parents more over it creates a good impression and love towards our parents that's Mom Dad and much more. It shows how much we care and love and live with them. It will also grow the readers loving level and over all moments and the co-authors have beautiful expressed, structured and presented.

This book is published under "Words Of Soul Publication" and Rahul B R is the compiler of this book called "Our First And Forever Love".

Acknowledgement

The completion of this book would not have been possible without the help of my parents, co-authors and friends and also publication too. I thank them whole heartedly for supporting and helping me in every step. So I am dedicating this book of mine to them...

प्रस्तावना

"हमारा पहला और हमेशा के लिए प्यार" पुस्तक माता-पिता के प्रति हमारे पहले प्यार की सुंदरता को और अधिक बढ़ा देती है, यह हमारे माता-पिता के प्रति एक अच्छी छाप और प्यार पैदा करती है जो कि मॉम डैड और बहुत कुछ है। यह दिखाता है कि हम उनकी कितनी परवाह करते हैं और प्यार करते हैं और उनके साथ रहते हैं। यह पाठकों के प्यार के स्तर और सभी क्षणों में भी बढ़ेगा और सह-लेखकों ने सुंदर व्यक्त, संरचित और प्रस्तुत किया है।

यह पुस्तक "वड्र्स ऑफ सोल पब्लिकेशन" के तहत प्रकाशित हुई है और "हमारा पहला और हमेशा के लिए प्यार" नामक इस पुस्तक के संकलनकर्ता राहुल बी आर हैं।

1. COMPILER OF THE BOOK

RAHUL B R

He was born in 19/09/1999 Ramanagara district, Karnataka.

But he is perceiving his higher studies in Bangalore. He has completed bachelor degree in science. He like to know more about literature and want to study more and more about it...

He started writing poems from past four years and he writes all kinds of poems... on life, about nature's beauty, love and much more. He is coauthored in many books, Compiler of the book called "The Song

Of Nature", "Nemophilist", "The Song Of Paradise", "Wings To Your Thoughts" and "The Unchosen Bond" and few more... and also his poems has been published in his college magazine too.

LOVE TOWARDS PARENTS

My love,

My only love...

It's my parents,

No one else...

They are my everything

And my all thing,

They are my inspiration

In all kinds of situation.

Love towards them will never end,

Because we share strong bond.

They are all time best,

In all types of worst.

My parents are prestigious

With lots of love and cares,

They help one another

To go ahead further.

Mother's carry their baby in the arms so that the baby
could see what she is seeing...

But Father's carry their baby on their shoulders so that the
baby could see beyond what he is seeing...

2. ANKITA NAHAR

#AKII#@@@ अंकिता नाहर मूल रूप से अजमेर, राजस्थान की रहने वाली हैं। ये लिखने के लिए हमेशा उत्साहित रहती है साथ ही हमेशा शब्दों से सुकून सा पाती हैं। ये अपने विचारों और जो भी इन्होंने अपनी जिंदगी से सीखा है, अनुभव लिया है उसे अपनी रचनाओं में लिख देती हैं। इससे इनकी रचनाएँ बहुत ही ज्यादा भावुक भावों वाली और प्रभावशाली बन जाती हैं। जो कि पढ़ने वालों को बहुत आकर्षित करती है। वह इस माध्यम को और आगे तक ले जाना चाहती हैं। आप इनकी रचनाओं को इंस्टाग्राम @naharankita1 पर पढ़ सकते हैं।

प्रिय माता पिता

जो मैंने कभी नहीं कहा आपसे वो आज मैं कहना चाहती हूं ।

कहना तो बहुत बार पहले भी चाहती थी पर कभी हिम्मत नहीं हो पाई।

आज जब मैं अपने बाबुल का आंगन छोड़ अपने पिया के घर जा रही हूं
तब जाकर इतनी हिम्मत आई हैं कि आप दोनों को कुछ बोल सकूं

हां माना अब मैं पिया के घर जाऊंगी,

पर अब भी पापा आपके पास कभी भी आ जाऊंगी

हां माना अब तक मुझसे गोल रोटी नहीं बनती

पर मम्मी कभी भी ससुराल से ताने नहीं लाऊंगी

हां माना पहले से काफी ज्यादा समझदार हो गई हूं

पर पापा अब भी आपके लिए नालायक बच्ची ही रहूंगी

हां माना जैसे में यहां भाई बहिनों से लड़ती थी,चिल्लाती थी

पर मम्मी मैं वैसे वहां नहीं करूंगी

सब से प्यार से बात करूंगी

हां माना बाबुल का घर भले ही छोड़ रही हूं

पर मम्मी पापा आप दोनों का हक हमेशा पहले जैसा ही रहेगा।

©AKII#@@@

3. KAVITA VIJAYWARGIYA

कविता विजयवर्गीय जो मध्यप्रदेश के गुना से संबंध रखती हैं। उन्हें सिंगिंग करना , लिखना , पढ़ना , बच्चों के साथ मस्ती करना ये सब बेहद पसंद है। धर्म से जुड़ी हर चीज , हर बात उन्हें आकर्षित करती है।

माता पिता बिन अधुरा जीवन

जिस तरह माता-पिता

अपने बच्चों के बिना अधुरे होते हैं ,

उसी तरह हम बच्चे भी तो

अपने माता पिता के बिना

कहां पूरे होते हैं !

दुनिया क्या कहेगी ये

माता पिता कहां मानते हैं

वो तो बस अपने

बच्चों की आंखों से आंसू चुरा कर

उनके लबों पर मुस्कराहट लाना जानते हैं !!

4. RIXIT MIDHA

रिक्षित मिढ़ा , राजस्थान, जयपुर के रहने वाले है। वह होटल मैनेजमेंट के छात्र और एक बढ़िया शेफ है। इनकी रूची लिखना, टेबल टेनिस खेलना और संगीत सुनना हैं।

रीक्षित जी ज्ञान लेने में तत्पर रहते हैं और इन्हें नए लोगो से मिलना बहुत पसंद है। यह पहले भी कई ऐन्थॉलॉजी के लेखक रह चुके है। ये कुछ नया करने दिखने का जज्बा रखने वाले एक होनहार युवक है।

संपर्क सूत्र IG:- r_write_emotions

जन्नत उर्फ मां

मेरी मां के आंचल में ही निकला है बचपन ,

उनसे ही जुड़ी है मेरी हर एक धड़कन ।

नहीं होना चाहता में उनसे होना कभी जुदा ,

क्यों की सही मायनों में तो वो ही है मेरा खुदा ।।

मां के साथ बीता हर एक पल मेरा अनमोल था ,

ना ही प्यार में मेरी मां के कभी कोई झोल था ।

मेरी मां के प्यार का ना ही कोई मोल

ओर रहूंगा सताता हमेशा कर के कलोल ।।

मां है मोहब्बत का नाम ,

मां को हजारों सलाम ।

कर दे फिदा अपनी जिंदगी ,

आए जो बच्चे का नाम ।।

मेरी मां मेरे लिए जन्नत का फूल है ,

प्यार उसे करना मेरा वसूल है ।

पूरी दुनिया की मोहब्बत मां की ममता के आगे फिजूल है ,

मां की हर दुआ मुझे कबूल है ।।

मां को नाराज़ करना मेरी सबसे बड़ी भूल है,

मां के क़दमों की मिट्टी तो जन्नत की धूल है ।।।

ओर आखिर में यही कहूंगा की!!

मां का कोई दिन नहीं होता

मां से हर एक दिन होता है।

5. MOHD. FARHAN ALAM LARI

इनका नाम मो॰ फरहान आलम लारी है। यह उत्तर-प्रदेश राज्य के रहने वाले है। इन्हें रब के हर फैसले पर पूरा भरोसा है। इनका कहना है कि, "बेशक है हर मुश्किल का हल, अगर रब से जुड़े रहे हर पल।"

इन्होंने कॉमर्स से पोस्ट-ग्रेजुएशन किया है और आजकल ये प्रतियोगी परीक्षाओं की तैयारी कर रहे है, और साथ ही साथ ये विधि छात्र भी है।

"माँ-बाप का प्यार, बेशुमार"

यह है प्यार, जब पहली बार गोद में था उठाया।

मेरे रोने पर, हर कोई था मुस्कुराया।।

यह है प्यार, जब पहली बार चलना सिखाया।

मेरे गिरने पर भी, हर कोई ताली बजाया।।

यह है प्यार, जब हुआ बीमार तो सब थे परेशान।

मेरे सिवा उन्हें, दिख ही न रहा था कोई इन्सान।।

यह है प्यार, जब रातों को शुरू करता था रोना।

मुश्किल हो जाता था,अक्सर उनका सोना।।

यह है प्यार, जब मेरे पीछे-पीछे घूमते थे लेकर खाना।

अभी भी उनके आगे मेरा, चलता न कोई बहाना।।

यह है प्यार, करते हैं मेरी हर ख्वाहिशों को पूरा।

बस छोड़ देते हैं अपने लिये हर कुछ अधूरा।।

यह है प्यार, कितनी मशक्कत और मोहब्बत से है पाला।

अक्सर खिला देते हैं, अपने मुँह का भी निवाला।।

यह है प्यार, गलती करने पर माँ का हमें समझाना।

फिर प्यार से हमें, देखकर खूब मुस्कुराना।।

यह है प्यार, जब कहता था मुझे स्कूल नहीं जाना।

माँ का काम था मेरी तरफ से सबको समझाना

यह है प्यार, पापा का शाम को घर वापस आना।

आते ही उनके पास जाना और प्यार से गले लगाना।।

यह है प्यार, एक बार में फोन का जवाब न मिलने पर बहुत घबराना।

तुरंत मेरे सभी दोस्तों से मेरा बारे में पता लगवाना।।

दुनिया में माँ-बाप के जैसा, नहीं कर सकता कोई प्यार।

यह है ऐसा प्यार, जिसका नहीं करता कोई इज़हार।।

खुशनसीब हो तुम जो मिला है, माँ-बाप का साया।

इन्हीं की दुआओं ने, तुम्हें हर मुसीबत से बचाया।।

क्योंकि ईंट से नहीं, माँ-बाप से बनता है परिवार।

अगर एक है छत, तो दूसरा है दीवार।।

6. VIYAYAMALATHI MANI

Vijayamalathi Mani pursuing her Master Degree in English Literature. She is a poetess, co compiler, Compiler. She engrossed in inking quotes and poetry. She is a pluviophile.Glance her musings on YQ @Violet vibes?.She wrote more than 3000 quotes on YQ. She has compiled 3 more anthologies. She received more than 250 e certificates in various competitions. She is the core member of Solaced pentales, World of Logophiles, Inner Souls. She has co-authored 500+ anthologies. She believes through

writings only can win other's.

IMPECCABLE TENDERNESS

Parents,

Visible Gods,

Impeccable lovers,

Real motivators,

Best friends,

Divine souls,

Everlasting love,

They pour towards their children,

Never hurt them,

Don't humiliate them,

Don't leave them,

They only live for their children,

They shed their blood,

Sacrifice their whole life,

For their children only,

You need not to present valuable gifts to them,

You need not to yield money to them,

But just keep them with you,

Just pour you love towards them,

All they want is just love,

Your love only!

7. SANA NOEL MURRAY

Sana Noel Murray is a 17 yr old student belonging from Nagpur Maharashtra, she's a writer, compiler and a motivational speaker.

MA & DAD MY ETERNAL BESTFRIENDS

29th April 2005, I was blessed to be called as the daughter of two of the most amazing people on the planet earth -My parents! My parents play multiple roles in my life they are my best friends, my Gurus and what not! Since I was a little girl I've always shared everything with them be it good or bad they have made me feel soo comfortable that I can literally open my heart and keep it in front of them. Rather than considering them as my parents I've always thought them to be my best friends we three go for outings, eat good food and have fun!

The times when I'm low, they motivate and encourage me to get out of it and tell me "it's nothing but a phase of life"

When I make a mistake, they correct me and guide me as my Gurus.

When I achieve the smallest thing, they are the ones who celebrate my success as of their own

Enjoying every single moment with them is a pure bilss, these two people are the reason of me being whatever I'm today without their love support and teachings nothing would've been possible.. Also in present times where friends are just made for a purpose. I know that no matter how many " Best friends" come and go these two people will always be standing Rock solid beside me in all my ups and downs ..

So here I'm celebrating 16 years of togetherness with my eternal best friends. Turning the pages to 16 and many more to go!

_Sana Murray

8. AASHIYA SUMAN

A poetess by passion and a shayara professionally. Proud introvert and a lover of loneliness. Loves penning her feelings. Paper has the best patience as everybody knows.

A BEST MOTHER

A best mother to the worst kid like me

She's the best personality I know till date

She always loves me more than I do to her

She's like a lucky luck,,to my unlucky fate

I Love you mumma..will love you till my last breath.

9. KAMINI PRADHAN

कामिनी प्रधान , पिता श्री मंगल प्रसाद प्रधान, माता श्रीमती तपोवंती प्रधान , जो ग्राम पंचायत- आमगांव, शाखा -तमनार ,जिला रायगढ़ छत्तीसगढ़ से रहने वाली है , जो अभी एम.एस. सी रसायन शास्त्र में अध्ययनरत है, जो पढ़ने , लिखने के साथ संगीत में रुचि रखती है ।

" पापा "

अपनी खुशियां छुपाए आग में तपते है ,

गर्मी के मौसम की गर्मी सहते है ,

बिना कुछ कहे अपनी इच्छाओं को दबा देते है ,

परिवार की जरूरतों में दिन रात एक कर देते है ,

वो आखों में सिकन दिखने तक नहीं देते ,

आखों की गहराई में छोटी बड़ी परेशानी छुआ देते है ,

दुनिया की बेहतरीन मूरत पापा की होती है ,

जो बचपन से हाथ पकड़ कर चलना सीखा देते है ,

गलत , सही मार्ग का परिचायक बन जाते है ,

उनसे बढ़कर कुछ नहीं जीवन में ,

पापा ही तो घर घर आंगन में ,

खुशियां पूरी होती है पापा की मेहरबानियां से ,

ये जीवन भी देखा मैने पापा की कुर्बानियों से ,

सास चलती है तो पापा सुकून को मिलता है ,

मेरी धड़कन के पल पल का हिसाब पापा को जाता है ,

बेहतर है वो जीवन में अपनी एक पहचान बनाए हुए ,

बेटी कहकर दिल से अपना पुकारते हुए ,

पापा का दर्जा दिया भगवान ने ,

मुझे अनमोल किस्सा बनाया पापा ने ।

© कामिनी प्रधान

10. DR. MAJOR NALINI JANARDHANAN

Dr (Major) Nalini Janardhanan, is a doctor who served in Indian Army as an Army Medical Officer She is a popular writer of Kerala who got Katha Award and a writer of many medical books for which she got IMA Sahithya Award. She is an Akashvani(All India Radio) and Doordarshan approved artist of Ghazals and Bhajans.

OUR PARENTS

Parents are our real treasure to be held close to our hearts. A father creates a firm foundation for his children. Being a friend, philosopher and guide, he teaches them values and etiquette. A father is a son's first hero. A daughter loves her father who considers her as a princess. Girls depend on their fathers for emotional and physical security. A mother has an important role in the family, taking care of the growth and development of children. Mothers protect children but fathers encourage them to take challenges helping to build confidence in them. Mothers stress upon sympathy, care and help. Both father and mother are equally important for a child. Both of them have equal roles to play as two pillars supporting the family. Under their care, children feel loved, protected and ready to face the challenges of the world.

But children should not forget the valuable contribution of their parents in their lives. They should not dump their parents in old age homes or throw them out of their homes to die like orphans on the streets. Children should look after their old parents when they need care and love in the last stages of their lives. The mantra from Taittriya Upanishad which says 'Matru Devo Bhava' (meaning: Honour your mother as God) and 'Pitru Devo Bhava' (meaning: Honour your father as God) is a valuable message for the present generation of children. We should respect our parents like Gods.

Dr Major Nalini Janardhanan

11. BINOD DAWADI

He is Binod Dawadi from Purano Naikap 13, Kathmandu, Nepal. He has completed his Master's Degree from Tribhuvan University in Major English. He likes to read and write literary forms. He has created many poems and stories. His hobbies are reading, writing, singing, watching movies, traveling, gardening, etc. Contact with her through mail
Mail : vinoddawadi9@gmail.com
What's APP : 9779860513496

LOVE TOWARDS PARENTS

I love you my parents,

I can't live without you,

You are my all thing,

You are my greatest treasure,

I can't give you,

Anything besides my love,

You are my all thing,

I can't be separated from you,

How much I love to you,

How can I show ?

©® Binod Dawadi

12. KASHISH SAXENA

Her name is Kashish Saxena. She is persuing mass communication . She loves to travel and explore different cultures and languages. Despite this, she loves cameras and want to peruse it as a profession.

PARENTS

When we feel down, who do we turn to find comfort?

When we feel hungry, who do we turn to find food to eat?

When we feel alone, who do we find to hold our hands?

There are the people whom we can't replace.

They are the one who gave we the face.

Ya, they nage in our works sometimes,

They scold us on our mistakes everytime.

But that too for our good life.

We can't deny the fact, parents can never be replaced.

Why to find love outside, when true love is waiting for you
our house everytime.

13. ANWESHA RATH

Anwesha Rath, A girl from small town used to see huge dreams now is working in anthologies is just 19 years old doing graduation her aim is just to take care of her parents as they cared for her till her dream is not writing poems but to share heartfelt message..

I REMEMBER

The day I meet you

Was the day you're unknown

But today you're my own

The relation started

And still lasted

The unknown person

Today become my close

I never knew

The partner I'll choose will you

To me you was just a stranger

But today for me you can face any danger

Today you're my family member

Now you are so close

That for you I develop

Today you are my part

From whom I never want to depart

The day from that till today

Each moment ,

I remember.

14. YAMUNA RAJAM

She is yamuna rajam from Port Blair,Andaman and Nicobar islands.She has completed her graduation in BSc Plant science from a recognized college JNRM and stenographer from ITI .Her hobbies are reading, interior décor ,writing ,gardening and a realistic content creator. She has contributed few essence of writeups in many publications.

A CUP OF WHOLE

My existence flowing in her vein

Remedies and sets of remembrance

Rare flower petal embrace a new bud

Her voice to my covered ear

About her spouse and grand ones

Belonging to mine in a new world

The only rythmic humming

Recognition by our heart beats .

After a months of cries and story time touched me, nesting
her arms.

The lord fight against the god

For elixir forgotten by the truth

The first blood and smile of

Immortal love blessed upon

The almighty eyes of mother.

15. KEERTHI PRIYA M

Keerthi is a passionate writer. Apart from writing she is an enthusiastic of travelling, gardening, playing chess, photography and art. She is a lover of history and psychology.

PARENTS LOVE

Parents' Love is pure,

Just like milk,

With the rhyme of care,

They keep us protected from every bad eye,

Parents are always special,

Every parent does everything for their children,

Over my whole life,

I have seen many parents struggling for their kids.

We spend most of the time with them,

We are nothing without them,

But at times we hate them when we feel our choices are
neglected,

Yet we should make them understand,

They would melt like ice at least for our happiness,

Parents' Love is always eternal.

16. VAISHVI AMIN

She is Vaishvi Amin . Contact with her through insta
id
insta: poems_life_

LOVE TOWARDS PARENTS

That dried rose on her table signifies love

Love that she left everything for

Fought against the dearest of all

And loved the one she hated once

The one with those hazel eyes

And a smile that fluttered her imagination

But the love was easy said then done

Her blue eyes sparkled like pearls from the ocean , When
he smiled at her

His laughs his talks were a addiction

That had her going crazy

But when the destiny was on their side

He wasn't

That rose was all that was left from the fire of love

But still she loved it like she loved him

Although the end was uncalled for

But the love played a role that none could have

The fight , the hate, the love didn't end the story

The destiny did

Still this love story had no end like tales we hear that is
why it is one of the unfinished one's

17. BISHAKHA KUMARI SAXENA

बिशाखा कुमारी सक्सेना जी ग्रेटर नोएडा की निवासी हैं और ये समाजशास्त्र में स्नातकोत्तर की उपाधि प्राप्त की हुई है । इनकी रूचि कुकिंग, कविता लेखन, पेंटिंग, फोटोग्राफी में है । इनकी लेखनी में मैगज़ीन और 100+ किताबों में इनकी रचनाये छप चुकी है।

दिल का थर्मामीटर

दिल के रूह से चाहती हूँ

तभी अपने दिल के थर्मामीटर से,

तुम्हारे प्यार को मापती हूँ ।

तुम्हारे अन्दर मुझसे चाहत की

कितने हद तक की शिद्दत है,

इसको तुम्हारे हर वार से तौलती हूँ।

जितनी मुझमें लगन है प्यार के लिए

उसी मनोभावों को तुम्हारे अन्दर,

पाने के लिए अपना दिल निकालकर रखती हूँ।

तुमहारी इतनी इबादत करती हूँ

तुमसे भी इसकी उम्मीद में ।

18. NILOFAR FAROOQUI TAUSEEF

नीलोफ़र फ़ारूक़ी तौसीफ़,बिहार शरीफ़, नालंदा में जन्मी और
पली-बढ़ी लेकिन मुंबई में रहती हैं। इन्होंने एम॰सी॰ए॰,
एम॰बी॰ए॰ किया है एवं आईटी में टीम लीडर पे कार्यरत हैं। अपने
विचारों एवं भावनाओं को अपनी लेखनी के माध्यम से पहचान
बनाना पसंद करती हैं। उनके लिए "लेखन क्रांति लाने के लिए एक
तलवार है"। 300 से अधिक पत्र-पत्रिकाओं में आलेख एवं शोध पत्र
मिले। देश के प्रतिष्ठित पत्र पत्रिकाओं में रचनाएँ प्रकाशित। आप
उनका fb और इंस्टाग्राम देख सकते हैं - @writernilofar

पहला प्यार

कली से फूल बनने का सफ़र, मुहब्बत का आगाज़।

पहली मुहब्बत, पहला नशा , नई-नई साज़।

विद्यालय में जब पहली बार नज़र मिली, दिल बेक़रार हुआ

मुस्कान छाई हर पल, मुझे पहला-पहला प्यार हुआ।

चुपके-चुपके करती इंतज़ार, दिल धड़कता बार-बार।

छुट्टी का दिन भाता ही नहीं, बेकार लगता था इतवार।

हर पल यादों में खोई रहती, सब समझते की सोई रहती।

मन ही मन शर्माती , रूह की आग़ोश में संजोई रहती।

सोंचती हूँ आज तुम मेरे बच्चे के पापा होते, मैं पत्नी होती

तुम मेरी पहली मुहब्बत होते, और मैं आखरीं होती।

19. HAR DEEPANSH BAHADUR SINHA

He is Har Deepansh Bahadur Sinha . He belongs to Lucknow,UP. He has done masters in Geography from National Post Graduate College. Completed his schooling from Study Hall. His hobbies are art , listening to music , cooking & loads of driving. His interest areas are Astronomy,Writing,Photography & Travelling a lot.

INSPIRING FROM THE STARTING

Parents are the biggest inspiration

They have got immense dedication,

There is a lot to admire

And too much to learn and inspire.

From day to night our father works hard

For his family he is the ultimate guard,

Any time any where he will sacrifice

For our happiness he won't compromise.

Dear mother is just like a kitchen in home

To keep us secured she might quit her comfort zone,

If there is limited food she will eat less

But serve you like as if it is limitless.

So we don't need to wander in seek of inspiration

Just look at them you will get the confirmation,

Their will is so courageous

Grasping from them is truly nutritious.

20. LAVENYA

She is Lavenya from karnal, Haryana,born on 31 March 2006 - daughter of Mr.Rajinder Kumar and Mrs.Himali Manik. Her age is 16 years and her rudimentary avocations are listening songs, studying especially science , making reels and writing. She have won awards in English declamation and writing skills.

IMMORTAL LOVE

Immortal means the thing which never dies . Love never decays , as like soul does not die . The purest love in this world is of mom and dad.Their love is selfless.Everyone loves us for a reason but mother,father love their child for no reason.It is truly said that even if we get seven lives we can't pay debt of mother and father.They are one who themselves suffer but don't make their children even face any difficulty.From born day of child to being adult,from walking to talking every moment for parents are special.They make us learn how to walk,talk and all things.Its being worst when you can't value your parents,when you say 'you don't know anything' or when you break their trust.They are one who made us come to this world,always love,value and respect them.They are true God on this earth.Rightly said by someone,in mother's father's feet,heaven exists.Mom and dad together make child's world beautiful.Without them children are incomplete as like they are incomplete without us.

21. BANASO KUMARI

Banaso Kumari is from jharkhand.She love to write.She is free spirit and nature lover.She love to write to express her hidden feelings.She believe that writing is directly connected to heart and is better to express her emotions. She have a such a creativity that she can write anything connected to real life and emotions.....she is little sensitive girl,she writes all her poems getting lesson from her life.She is a author of her solo book name 'So Many Things To Say' .

DAD LOVE

You have loved me and held my hand,

Since my birth.

There is no better daddy in all the earth .

I am princess not because I have a prince,

But because my father is a king.

I will watch you as you guide me through life

With you,I will be able to handle any string.

A little girl needs her daddy to love her,

With gentlemanly charm,

To hold her tightly when she is afraid

And keeps her safe from harm.

Father's daughters a timeless bond,

Vaster than oceans ,tranquil as ponds

My handprint and handmade art,

Is for you to know

You are always in my heart.

22. HENA NOOR AAIN

Her name is Hena Noor Aain she live in Kolkata she completed her graduation in history honour she started writing since in class 4 when she first time read Mirza Ghalib shayari That inspired her a lot she love to write and read books writing which make me hope in difficult times

LOVE TOWARDS PARENTS

Love toward parents is like a beauty of life

Because they remind you true love exist in this world

Love toward parent is like a nature Beauty

which give you happiness in difficult times

But never make you feel sad

Love toward parents mean a heart of life

which give you long lasting happiness .

23. SHAISTA FALAK NAAZ

इनका नाम शाइस्ता फलक नाज़ है ।ओडिशा की रहने वाली लेखिका शाइस्ता फलक नाज़ 10वीं पढ़ रहे इतारुल हक और चमन आरा की बेटी हैं और उन्होंने अभी-अभी लेखन की दुनिया में शुरुआत की है।

मां-पापा

माँ पापा, आप दोनो कोई फरिश्ता तो नहीं?

क्यूंकि आपके साथ जैसा यहां कोई रिश्ता नहीं।

इस मतलब की दुनिया में, बस आप दोनो बेमतलब का प्यार कर सकते हो,

हमसे बिना कुछ मांगे, अपनी पूरी जिंदगी हमारे नाम कर सकते हो |

आप दोनो कैसे कर लेते हो सब कुछ?

माँ पापा, आप कोई सपना तो नहीं?

क्यूंकी आप दोनो सा यहां कोई अपना नहीं।

खुदा ने मुझे माँ बाप दिए हैं, और जिंदगी से क्या मांगू ?

उनके बगैर तो ये ज़िंदगी भी बेकार है,

मुझसे ज्यादा खुशनसीब कौन होगा, मेरे पास मेरे माँ बाप का प्यार है।

दुनिया वाले तोलते हैं अमीरी पैसों के नाम पे,

पर वो नहीं जानते, सबसे बड़ी दौलत तो माँ पापा का साथ है,

उनके साथ के साथ तो, ठंड भी सुकून और धूप भी बरसात है।

माँ बाप के बिना ये जिंदगी कैसी होती,

अब तो ये सोचने की भी हिम्मत नहीं होती,

बस युंही उन्हें एक नज़र प्यार से देख लिया करो,

क्यूंकी सबके नसीब में हज नहीं होती।

ऐ खुदा, इतना किस्मतवाला बनाया है मुझे

इस लायक भी बनाना, के अपने माँ बाप की हर ख़्वाहइश, हर ख़ुशी, हर चाहत को पुरा कर सकुं,

बस इतना सिखाना।

माँ पापा, आपकी गोद में सारी तक्लीफें खतम हो जाती हैं,

वो कुछ सुकून के पल, जिंदगी भर याद रह जाती हैं,

आपकी हसी से हमारी मुश्किलें दूर हो जाती हैं,

ऐसा क्या जादू है आप दोनो में, जो हर चीज़ बेहतरीन हो जाती हैं।

माँ पापा, आपकी आँखें में नूर और चेहरा रूहानी है

आप दोनो को देख, यकीन है आता के सच धरती पे स्वर्ग की कहानी है,

आप दोनो के साथ आसन हर परेशानी है,

माँ पापा, हम से तुम नहीं, तुमसे हमारी जिंदगानी है।

24. MARIA SHAIKH

"She is a girl with emotions,
Fake expressions with true resolutions,
When you look into her heart,
You will find a kind soul,
When you look into her eyes,
You can find an expression of love...

TREE OF LOVE

My family is a tree,

You are its root,

You show me happiness always free..

If oxygen is the way to live,

You are my O2,

I know you love me

I love you too..

The tree can not stand without root,

I hope you understand,

Never leave us as we are your shoot..

The day I screamed for the first time,

I knew how greedy you are for me,

On my tears you made me smile..

It's only you who can do,

In your pain to smile and hide the real you..

You impersonate as a happy man,

I know you were not happy, but my first cry says now you
can..

You lived yourself in me,

I am a part of you,

And I want myself you to be..

25. KAJARI GUHA

Kajari Guha is a published author of several books.She is a poetess,composer and a connoisseur of art.She is a translator too.She has command over three languages -English,Bengali and Hindi.

PARENTAL LOVE !

Priceless and patient!

Rhapsody of complacence!

Parental love is

Like a soft feather

With healing touch

After the sultry weather!

Free from any expectation

Parental love fills you

With all admiration!

The tree with a

Shady bower

It saves you from

The scorching summer!

Like a ripple with

A murmuring tone

It creates an aura of

A soothing drone

Of bees humming

A tune of ecstasy

That takes you to the

Land of love

Sans any jealousy!

26. BHOOMIKA SHARMA

Bhoomika Sharma,a teacher and a profound thinker and writer.she is published Writer of book- In search of happiness- Reality of life ans Saanso Ki Sargam(Kavya Saklan).She wrote in many anthologies as a co-author. She writes in both the languages Hindi and English.

TRUE BOND OF LOVE-A LIFE-MAKER-PARENTS

A relationship very strong,

Which remain with us for long.

All closeness and proximity,

They are life agility.

A True shade of happiness,

All my life in their shade full of cheerfulness.

An enlightened lamp lit my life with truth,

Taught me all patience and faith.

A Life of truth and sincere honesty,

I learnt from them all sublimity.

Filled with joy , glee and gaiety,

My life with you is joyous glittery and morality.

You with good spirit taught me reality,

I learn a lesson of responsibility.

You gave me path of reverence,

I learnt a lesson of preference.

You became a good torch-bearer,

I learnt to be truthful and sincere.

You in my life is a personality of royal,

Taught me a lesson to be loyal.

You give me path of serenity,

My life peaceful with capability.

You are only like precious pearls,

All gems on life Shining and clear.

You are everything I , my life for life-maker,

You are my wondrous future-builder.

- Bhoomika Sharma

27. SALMA KHAN

Salma khan is from Indore. Her graduated from Devi Ahilya Vishwavidyalaya Indore. Her hobbies are reading - writing ✍?, painting & singing. Keep naturals & creative thoughts. She's started writing in month of October 2021. Her thoughts are part of co-author in many anthologies .

KEEP RESPECT OUR PARENTS

1. The world's purest love is that of mother and father…

Everything else is infatuation….

2. May God keep my mother and father safe always….

Even if you deprive me of wealth, but don't do it with the shadow of my father and mother.

3. To love the parents

It's hard to write in words…

Every feeling of their love is different.

4. Parents are perfect personalities…..

In whose shadow we rule…

5. Even parents raise 5 children with the same love…

But in today's time even 5 children together are not able to take care of their parents..

6. Shame on those people…..

Those who leave their old parents in old age homes….

7. We respect our parents less

In front of their sacrifices......

28. RITU GUPTA

ऋत्ज़@ डॉ ऋतु, एक शिक्षिका, एक काउंसिलर के अलावा यह एक लेखिका तथा समाज सेविका भी हैं। इनकी एकारचन,"अ प्लेस इन द सन", "हश्ड ऐंगुइश" तथा "द प्रिमरोज़ आईल" को काफी मान भी प्राप्त हुआ है। आपने शिक्षा जगत तथा समाज में अपनी एक पहचान बनाई है। फोटोग्राफी, संगीत, नृत्य, भ्रमण इनकी रूचि है। इनकी उपलब्धियों के कारण, "इंकज़ोयड बुक आफ रिकाइड्स" में इनका नाम दर्ज किया गया है। शिक्षा के क्षेत्र में- "इंटरनैशनल स्कूल अवार्ड", "किरणमयी अवार्ड" एवं "राष्ट्रीय शिक्षा रत्न सम्मान" से इन्हें सम्मानित किया गया है।

माता-पिता - जीवन का सार

पिता वो पेड़ है, जिनकी छाया शीतल होती है,

वो उजाला है, जो जीवन पथ दर्शाती है ।

माँ यदि धरा है, तो पिता हैं गगन, जो..

बच्चों की भलाई के लिए, हजार करे जतन।

किस्मत वाले हैं जिनके सर पर, माता-पिता का हाथ होता है,

हर ज़िद पूरी होती है उनकी, जब माता-पिता का साथ होता है।

जो कदम डगमगाए, तो हाथ पकड़ लेते हैं,

माता-पिता वो फरिश्ता हैं, जो हमें, हमेशा संभाल लेते हैं।

विश्वास के पंख देकर, कहते हैं- "भरो उड़ान"..

गिरना संभलना, यही तो है असली शान

शासन में भी प्यार झलकता, उनके हर एक बात से,

खामोशी से स्वयं जूझते, अनचाहे हालात से।

रक्षा कवच बनकर जो, अडिग रहे तूफानों में

नमन ऐसे माता-पिता को, जिनकी गिनती हो भगवानों में।

29. MANISHA HALDAR

Manisha Haldar is the Writer , Poetess , Pranic Healer and would be Doctor from the Madhya Pradesh , India. She writes to spread peace and love.

PARENTS

Our parents are the first and forever love of us.

Our love begins with parents.

And parents love us truly.

Love is incomplete without parents.

Life is full of love because of our parents only.

Parents are our life.

Parents are our world.

They create our world full of love.

If parents are not with us.

Our life and world become without love.

Our life will become incomplete.

Our parents complete us.

We all are from our parents.

And our parents are from their parents.

Our parents are from us.

30. SATYABHAMA PRADHAN

सत्यभामा प्रधान जो एक कवियत्री है जो की ओड़िशा निवासी है ।
ये जिंदगी और प्रकृति से जुड़े लेख लिखने में दिलचस्पी रखती है।
इनसे संपर्क करने के लिये जुड़े।
Insta I'd @pardhan_satyabhama

बनकर छाँव ...

बनकर छाँव कड़ी धूप से जो हमें बचाते हैं,

हमारी मुस्कुराहट से अपने सारे गम भुल जाते हैं,

नन्हे परिन्दों के लिए खुला आसमान जो बन जाते हैं,

बनकर दुसरी भगवान इस धरती पर

माता-पिता वो कहलाते हैं।

31. SANJAY SHARMA

संजय शर्मा ,,, देहरादून उत्तराखंड के रहने वाले है ,, प्रॉपर्टी और मेडिसिन के व्यापार में व्यस्त रहने वाले सफल कारोबारी है । इनकी रुची लिखना,, लॉन्ग ड्राइव ,, पहाड़ों पर घूमना ,,दोस्त बनाना दोस्तो के साथ मस्ती करना के साथ साथ धार्मिक स्थल पर जाना और ईश्वर के प्रति आस्था अत्यधिक पसंद है ,,लिखना आज भी यदि कोई तस्वीर सामने आ जाए तो शब्द जुड़ते चले जाते है और लिखने को प्रेरित करते है ऐसे इनका लेखन शुरू हुआ।

माता - पिता

माता पिता से मेरे रिश्ते का गणित

कितना सरल रहा,

फिर भी कितना जटिल....

माता पिता मुझे अपना सुख

बाँटने के लिए चाहते रहे....

और मैं उनको....

दुःख बाँटने के लिए.....